This Book is Pres

Peggy Kellom

By

Marian Hedger

On

June 2003

Treasures
of
Darkness

Poems to lift your spirit to
God in life's dark hours

by

Marian E. Pledger

WHOLENESS PUBLICATIONS
CANTON ✝ OHIO

ISBN 1-893042-07-3

Wholeness Publications
P.O. Box 20362, Canton, Ohio 44701
(330) 455-3663

Scripture portions in this book are from the
King James Version.

Wholeness Publications offers special discounts for bulk purchases of its products to be used for fund-raising, premium gifts, sales promotions, educational use, etc. Book excerpts or special editions can be produced to specification. For information contact the Special Sales Department at the above address.

Printed in the United States of America

"And I will give thee the treasures of darkness,
And hidden riches of secret places,
That thou mayest know that I, the LORD,
Which call thee by thy name, am the God of Israel."

Isaiah 45:3

Part

1

LIFE

SALVATION

Thou art my hiding place and my shield: I hope in thy word.
Psalm 119:114

IN CHRIST WE BELIEVE

My Hiding Place

When life is more than you can bear.
When burdens grow too large to share
With fellow humans here below.
I know a place where you can go.

When doubts and tears grip your soul.
When to your hopes it's hard to hold.
When you have done your very best.
I know a place where you can rest.

When friends forsake and loved ones too.
When you just don't know what to do.
When you can see no sign of release.
I know a place of perfect peace.

When you seem to be marching to a different beat
From nearly all others in life you meet.
When troubles are coming on every hand.
I know a place in a peaceful land.

You simply stop all your activities.
And falling down on bended knees,
You run, in prayer, to your God above,
Who'll recharge you with His matchless love.

You pour your heart out to Him and find
You never get a busy signal on His phone line.
You meditate on His Word and see
How comforting He can be.

You listen to what He says as you pray.
You know He will never go away.
For He has said, "I'll never leave or forsake."
So, you give Him all your burdens and heartaches.

In turn, He gives you His perfect peace.
And believing His Word, You'll find release
From all that caused your head to hang low
And your aching heart to so rapidly go.

He is your faithful HIDING PLACE –
Your strong, secure, protected space,
Where you can run when you've done your best
And know your soul will find needed rest.

He is your shelter from life's many storms.
Your sun, your peace, when a dark cloud forms.
Refueled by His amazing grace,
You'll gain new strength to run this race.

SALVATION

My times are in thy hand: de-liver me from the hand of mine enemies, and from them that persecute me.

Psalm 31:15

IN CHRIST WE BELIEVE

My Times

My times are in thy hand, dear Lord.
No safer place could I be.
I just need to keep my eyes on you,
And trust you to keep guiding me.

SALVATION

Take therefore no thought for the morrow: for the morrow shall take thought for the things of itself. Sufficient unto the day is the evil thereof.

Matthew
6:34

IN CHRIST WE BELIEVE

Just Today

There are two days of each week I can do nothing
about:
Yesterday with its sorrows,
And tomorrow with its doubts.
So help me live just today, Lord,
In the center of your will.
Use me to bless those around me,
And keep my anxious heart still.

SALVATION

If the world hate you, ye know that it hated me before it hated you.

John 15:18

IN CHRIST WE BELIEVE

Fruit

Father, help me to so live my life,
That when my fruit the people see,
They'll glorify you in worshipful praise,
'Cause they'll see you reflected in me.

SALVATION

O give thanks unto the Lord,
for he is good: for his mercy
endureth for ever.
Psalm 107:1

IN CHRIST WE BELIEVE

Thanksgiving

Whatever happened to Thanksgiving?
It seems to have passed away.
People go from celebrating Halloween,
To shopping for Christmas Day.

Whatever happened to Thanksgiving?
This day was set aside
For giving thanks to God Almighty,
Whose loving kindness can not be denied.

For who else would continue to bless
With sun and rain and life,
A people so stiff-necked and self-seeking,
Who destroy His world with hatred and strife?

Who else would continue to reach out
With a steadfast heart of love,
To such rebellious, ungrateful people
Who deny His Lordship above.

Dear Lord, bring back Thanksgiving.
Fill our hearts with gratitude to you.
For every good and perfect gift
Comes down from you, 'tis true.

My Reward

"Well done thou good and faithful servant,"
My Master may not say to me.
For I've not been so very good,
And often faithless I seem to be.

But peace will fill my soul,
And rejoice I surely would,
If He'd say of me what He said of Mary,
"She hath done what she could."

SALVATION

Matthew
20:1,2

IN CHRIST WE BELIEVE

For the kingdom of heaven is like unto a man that is an householder, which went out early in the morning to hire labourers into his vineyard.

And when he had agreed with the labourers for a penny a day, he sent them into his vineyard.

His Penny

Money, money, money,
That's all some folks holler.
Seems like they'll do most anything
To gain another dollar.

But I've decided to invest my life
In serving the many, many,
God brings across my path each day,
And be satisfied with His penny.

For a penny is what He promised those
Who'd serve in His vineyard
To get a penny from the God of Grace,
Is not so very hard.

For He hires children, teens,
Adults, and seniors too.
You can even come on your death bed,
And He'll give His penny to you.

This penny from the King of Eternity,
You can take to heaven with you.
Yes, I'd rather have it than all the money
I have to leave when my life's through.

O God, thou hast taught me from my youth: and hitherto have I declared thy wondrous works.

Now also when I am old and greyheaded, O God, forsake me not; until I have shewed thy strength unto this generation and thy power to every one that is to come.

My Secret for Healthy Aging

My secret for healthy aging,
I'll gladly share with you.
Use it daily in your life,
And you'll surely find it's true.

The killers of worry, stress and regret
Can't get you down as your age goes up,
If you always see your life as
A half-full, not half-empty cup.

Count your blessings daily –
Noting the things that you can do
To be a blessing in someone's life –
Helping them not to be so blue.

Don't focus on what you have lost
Of your physique, your hair or speed.
Focus on what you yet have left
To help meet another person's need.

For it's fretting about the things
That used to be, you see,
That robs your life and mine
Of good health and vitality.

Can you walk, or drive a car?
Then go visit some lonely soul.
If you can talk, call a hurting one
And help warm a heart grown cold.

Give a gift to a needy soul.
Send a cheerful card or a letter.
A prayer you whisper in the night
Can make someone's life quite better.

Just smile, if you can't walk or talk.
Or simply give a friendly hand wave.
Often the ones around who are younger and fair
Are closer than you to the grave.

It's true that around you are those
Who have much more than you do.
If you concentrate on them,
Your healthy days will be few.

Think of the ones who have less
Than God has blessed you to possess.
If you use what you've got to help others,
These days can be your very best.

Yes – thankfully thinking of others
Is my secret to aging in a healthy way.
Keep a lookout for someone less fortunate
And do something to bless their day.

Part

2

OUR TIMES

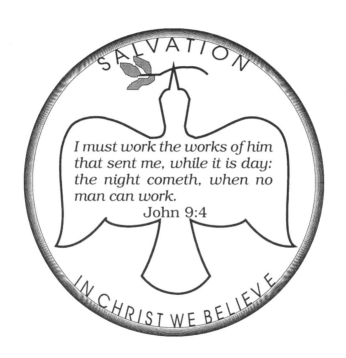

SALVATION

I must work the works of him that sent me, while it is day: the night cometh, when no man can work.

John 9:4

IN CHRIST WE BELIEVE

Working While It's Day

I was born and raised in the good old U.S.A.
Its citizen I'm proud to be.
But this God-blessed land of my abode
Has become a strange place to me.

Unborn, innocent children killed –
All legal, in the name of choices;
Profanity and perversions beyond belief
Flooding the media with filthy voices.

Oh, Lord, send a revival! Send it today!
Move your people to be the salt and the light.
We must quickly get busy doing your will,
'Cause it looks like it'll soon be night.

SALVATION

Remembering mine affliction
and my misery, the worm-
wood and the gall.
Lamentations 3:19

IN CHRIST WE BELIEVE

My Son

He used to come
    this son of mine.
I'd look up and see
    him most anytime.
"Hi, Ma," he'd say,
    with an engaging smile.
Sometimes he'd sit
    and chat awhile
He used to come.

He used to call,
    this son of mine.
"Hi, Ma," he'd say.
    "Everything's OK."

"I'll probably stop by
  after work today."
He used to call.

Now he doesn't come
  and he doesn't call.
I don't hear a word
  from him at all.
Where is this child
  I bounced on my knee;
Who into a handsome man
  grew to be?
How is he, this one
  who's my pride and joy?

My hopes, my dreams,
      are wrapped up in this boy.

Oh, dear merciful Lord
      who controls all from above,
Please tell my son
      of my unfailing love.
Please let him know
      that I really do care.
Like You, for him,
      I'll always be there.
Give him Your strength
      to run this race.

Help him to find
    in this world, his place.
Be his Rock. Be his Shield.
    Be His Hiding Place.
When life beats him down,
    sustain him by Your grace.

Let him not forget You -
    his God above.
Let him not forget
    his mother's love.
Everything's possible with You -
    Please tell him for me.
I'll just remember prayerful
    and patient to be.

As You work out Your wonderful
        plan for his life.
Please give him a godly
        and helpful wife.
Perhaps, one day, to the door
        or telephone I'll run,
And find myself again
        talking with my dear son.

Released

Released into the hands of God.
Released into His loving care.
This child I conceived, nurtured and bore,
I leave him confidently there.

My best I did to guide him
    with my motherly prayers and love.
My best I did to teach him
    with wisdom from God above.

Freely sacrificed I,
    my personal wants and desires;
Striving to plant within his heart
    the saving Heavenly Fire.

Release him now I do,
　　　into this sea of life.
I place him in my basket
　　　with love and prayers made tight.

Let me not snatch him back, dear Lord.
Let me not worry or fret.
For you are the sovereign, faithful God.
You are watching over him yet.

Lead someone to him, precious Lord,
　　　to help him be what you want him to be.
Let him not crawl out of his basket,
　　　and be destroyed by this raging sea.

Help him one day to know
    his loving mom did all she could do,
To train him in the way he should go,
    and to your Word be true.

Give him a love for you, Father,
    and a hunger to live by your truths too.
I sure want to greet my child
    When, at last, I'm in Heaven with you.

SALVATION

Train up a child in the way he should go: and when he is old, he will not depart from it.
Proverbs 22:6

IN CHRIST WE BELIEVE

Our Children

Lord, save our children, save our youth,
My troubled soul cries today.
Look at what they're becoming and doing.
So far from you they do stray.

I can save the children and the youth too,
Our Lord to me answered back.
I am the Almighty, All-knowing God –
Able to rescue all from Satanic attack.

But I choose to work through people.
The Church is my instrument on earth.
Whom can I send? Who will go for us;
To bring these young ones to new birth?

Lord, send a revival. Please send a revival.
Revive your Church, I do pray.
For we've drifted away from the foundation laid.
So very far from your heart are we today.

Give me your life for the children and youth,
Our Lord requested of me.
I'll use you to nurture these seedlings with care.
Psalm 1 trees they yet can be.

I will open my mouth in a parable: I will utter dark sayings of old:

Which we have heard and known, and our fathers have told us.

We will not hide them from their children, shewing to the generation to come the praises of the Lord, and his strength, and his wonderful works that he hath done.

Passing It On

African-American child, don't you know,
Of all the people who so long ago,
Struggled and saved,
And worked and gave,
That you might live and grow?

With pride, grab their baton of faith.
With joy, run your leg of the race.
If you let God be your guide,
And keep the Bible by your side,
Then you'll be a winner, I know.

Forgotten

What has happened to us?
How could we fall so low?
We were such a proud, achieving people
Not so very long ago.

What has happened to us?
My aching heart breaks as I see
The lack of love and lost work ethic
That fills life all around me.

Brought to America as slaves,
We were hopeless and weak.
But, with faith in God and each other,
We got on our feet.

We were people of integrity.
We were honest and clean,
Though holes filled our shoes,
And tattered were our blue jeans.

We valued the church and the Bible.
An education was greatly prized too.
"Be your best," was our motto.
"To your upbringing be true."

Our heroes were Jackie Robinson,
Mary Bethune and the rest
Who drank deeply life's sorrows
And still gave their very best.

Our elders were respected.
Family life was prized too.
Children were highly valued and precious.
In prison we had just a few.

Each generation aspired
To go beyond the last.
Climbing higher the success ladder,
Breaking all records of the past.

What has happened to us?
Could it possibly be
That we've forgotten to pass on
Our proud history?

Drug addictions and abortions,
Smart mouth kids with drooping pants.
Some call this black identity.
I say, "No way! No chance!"

Oh, my beloved black people, go back.
Uncover the old paths and see.
A proud respected people
We can return to be.

Oh, my dark people, go back,
To where we lost our way.
Back to God, back to church,
Back to family, while it's yet day.

For the night surely is coming
When God's wrath will fall
On each who knew His will
And did it not at all.

Tell our story to the children.
Let them know what God has done.
Tell the sacrifices of the past
That made possible their present fun.

It took faith in God and hard work
To stand us tall upon our feet.
It will yet take these too
If this world system we're to beat.

It is not too late, my people.
God is still upon His throne.
Return to Him in sincere prayer.
He can yet make us strong.

SALVATION

Psalm
78:6,7

IN CHRIST WE BELIEVE

That the generation to come might know them, even the children which should be born; who should arise and declare them to their children:

That they might set their hope in God, and not forget the works of God, but keep his commandments:

Them

Sometimes, I think about them –
    the people who paved the way for me
       with their blood,
          their sweat,
             and their tears.

I see them in hot, beautiful West Africa,
    singing, dancing,
       sowing, reaping,
         happy, proud,
           marrying and giving birth.

Yes, sometimes I think about them.

Sometimes I think about them –
the ones who lived before me.
I see them bewildered, confused, hurt,
broken,
sick as they board the slave ships
- lonely, sad,
weeping,
broken-hearted.

I see them landing on this American shore
to labor without reward,
to build houses for others to enjoy,
to till another's soil –
nurse another's babies.

I see them reach out and embrace the God who sets
slaves free.
    Husbands taken –
        children too,
           but God's always there.

From their enslaved bodies come His songs,
    from hearts he has set free.

Yes, sometimes I think about them.

Sometimes I think about them - - -
    the ones who when freed found themselves
    still slaves because

they had no education - - -
                couldn't read, write - - -
                    no money.

Nothing much to do but return to the old master
again –
        sharecropping,
            washing,
                ironing,
                    still enslaved.

My heart fills with pride as I remember how they
        loved each other,
                taught themselves to read and write,
                    shared, stuck together,

dreamed dreams for me,
>> worked hard to cut a path for me,
>> build a future for me,
>> open doors for me.

My joy overflows as I see them overcoming segregation,
Jim Crow, discrimination –
>> achieving against all odds,
>> starting schools, colleges, businesses –
>> trusting in their God and
>> sticking together.

Yes, - - - Sometimes I think about them.
I wonder if they could see, - - -
WHAT WOULD THEY THINK ABOUT YOU AND ME?

Part

3

THE
AFTER LIFE

Bearing Another's Burdens

I wish that I could sit with you today,
To share with you your heartache and your pain;
To grieve with you in silence, as you think
Of your precious one who is now heaven's gain

I wish that I could gently touch your hand –
Just by my very presence shout I care,
About your agony and grievous loss –
About the heavy burden you now must bear

Some noble, comforting deed I'd gladly do.
Her homegoing has left such emptiness.
But only our wise, almighty, loving God
Can see you victoriously through this great test.

For it is He who chose to leave you laboring here,
And call your loving, gracious mother home.
He only can fill her now empty great shoes,
And let you know that you are not alone.

A test of faith in Him this surely is.
A test of faith in His wisdom, grace, and love;
To leave you here still to run your race,
And call her to live with Him above.

But you must labor on in His vineyard.
One day He will call your name too.
Then you will be reunited with your loved one,
Because your earthly work will also be through.

I said in mine heart concerning the estate of the sons of men, that God might manifest them, and that they might see that they themselves are beasts.

The Day That Susan Died

Where does the life of a little kitty go,
When she ceases to frolic down here below?

Does it simply evaporate into the air?
Or does it travel on to some place, somewhere?

Please tell me, God.
I want to know.
Where does the life of a little kitty go.

Brethren, I count not myself to have apprehended: but this one thing I do, forgetting those things which are behind, and reaching forth unto those things which are before,

I press toward the mark for the prize of the high calling of God in Christ Jesus.

Pressing On

Her earthly work was done, so she retired.
Promoted from labor to reward, she moved up higher.
With grateful hearts, we thank God for her life,
And Bless His name for giving you such a wife.

We wipe our eyes and press on while it's day.
There absolutely is no other way!
So press on until your victor's crown is won.
And you hear our Heavenly Father say, "Well done."

SALVATION

I have fought a good fight, I have finished my course, I have kept the faith:
II Timothy 4:7

IN CHRIST WE BELIEVE

A Faithful Soldier

She fought a good fight.
She finished her course.
She kept the faith.
She ran well her leg of the race.

The crown has been won.
The white gown has been don.
The "Well done" has been said.
She is in a far better place.

She's singing up there.
Somewhere in the air
With that Heavenly choir.
I can hear her, can't you?

Heaven won't be the same
Since she became its gain
Escaping this world of pain.
We'll join her one day too.

SALVATION

Precious in the sight of the Lord is the death of his saints.
Psalms 116:15

IN CHRIST WE BELIEVE

Home At Last

I'm home. I'm home at last! O Happy Day!
Our loving Lord has wiped all my tears away.
Now that I'm gone, do not grieve for me.
I am exactly where I want to be.
Finally finished with this world of grief and pain,
I've been called home, my gown and crown to gain.
I'm with my blessed Lord who saw me through.
Everything about me is all so very new.
I'm free – I'm free at last, by His grace.
I've finished my course – I ran well my leg of the race.
Now you must take the baton I passed to you,
And run your leg as I'd expect you to do.

SALVATION

And the things that thou hast heard of me among many witnesses, the same commit thou to faithful men, who shall be able to teach others also.

II Timothy
2:2

IN CHRIST WE BELIEVE

My Last Will And Testament

To all God blesses me to touch with my life.

I don't have money or fine earthly possessions to leave you. But prayerfully, with full confidence that God is able to deliver all to you...

I leave you **faith in God**. No matter what life gives you, with this faith, you will be a victorious over comer. Remember there is a sovereign, all-powerful, loving God who is able to work all things together for your good. - Faith in your fellowman. There are still some godly people in this world. - Faith in yourself. Be a dreamer. You with God are a majority.

I leave you **hope**. There is no sorrow heaven can not feel. There is no pain our Christ can not relieve. There is no burden He'll not help you bear. Life is never a cave when you have your hope in Christ, but a series of tunnels. God will always make a way for His children.

I leave you **love**. - Love for yourself, love for your fellow man, love for God. No one can conquer the power of love, for love seeks only to fulfill the needs of others with no thought for self.

I leave you **confidence** in your ability to be used by God to impact this world for good and for His glory. When God wants to impact this world for good, He never calls a committee meeting, but one person who will step out, in faith, on His Word. Always remember that you can be this one person. You can't do everything, but you can do something. What you can do, by God's grace, DO IT!!

I leave you **commitment** to strive every day to be the best you can be in all you attempt. - Commitment to do all you can to help our young people to be all they can be.

I leave you a **strong work ethic**. Success is 10% inspiration and 90% perspiration. Don't be afraid of hard work. No success is sweeter than that which comes after much hard work, sweat and tears.

I leave you **knowledge** of the sovereignty of God. The sovereignty of God is the single impregnable rock to which the human soul can cling throughout the storms of life. No matter how bad things look and are, our loving Heavenly Father is always in control.

I leave you **respect**. - Respect for yourself, your family, your nation and your God. Always remember whose your are, where you have come from, and who you are. You are an ambassador for Christ. You are a descendant of a long line of hard-working, brilliant people. You are not your own. You have been bought with a price. You can not ever "do your own thing." You must always do "His thing." You are not a single blade of grass but a link in a long, continuous chain that started with God and ends with Him.

I leave you **determination**. Never give up striving to walk closely with God. No failure is final unless you give up.

I leave you **joy unspeakable**. - The joy that fills to over-flowing those who know that they are in the will of God.

I leave you a **hunger to know God** intimately. - To live daily in the consciousness of His presence. May your hunger for Him be so great that you will never be satisfied with the things this world has to offer.

I leave you a **burning desire** to keep pressing toward the mark for the prize. Never focus on what you have lost, but what you have left. Never focus on your defeats, but where you go from here. Never focus on the broken pieces of your life, but on the One who can take the broken pieces and shape a new trophy for His honor and glory.

I leave you a **goal**. Always be happy to gladly spend your life and be spent for our Lord. - To be broken bread and poured out wine. - To be used by God to share the knowledge of Him and our Christ with as many as you can in your lifetime. - To take as many to Heaven with you as you can.

I leave you **racial pride**. Always be satisfied to be you. Every group of people has those of whom they are not proud and of whom they can not speak well. But always accent the positive. Don't bad-mouth your people. There is always something good, something lovely, something of good report, something virtuous to think on and to share. Look for the good in each person and praise this. You have a rich heritage of creative, intelligent, hard-working, law-abiding, God-fearing, persistent, proud people. Live in the light of this richness.

I leave you belief in the **power of prayer**. The eyes of our Lord are upon the righteous and His ears are always open to their cry. Obey God. Talk with Him about everything and trust Him to do what is best. Much will come up in your life about which you can do little or nothing. But talk to your all-powerful Heavenly Father. He can...He will fight your battles. So, let Him.

Finally, I leave you **rest**. The rest that comes to the weary, war-worn soldier when the Commanding Officer – the King of Kings – says, "Come home, my child. You have done what you could."

About The Author

Marian Pledger is a full-time Christian missionary teacher and speaker committed mainly to evangelizing and discipling children and women. She is a graduate of Miami University of Ohio, Cleveland State University, the Child Evangelism Fellowship Leadership Training Institute, and the West Africa Leadership Training Institute. She is an instructor at the Progressive Baptist Bible Institute, an extension unit of the American Baptist College in Nashville, Tennessee. Other publications by Marian Pledger include, The Black Thread: An account of the Biblical heritage of Black people in the language of the common man.